The Visual Gu

Asperger's Syndrome: Social Energy (1)

by Alis Rowe

Also by Alis Rowe

One Lonely Mind
978-0-9562693-0-0

The Girl with the Curly Hair - Asperger's and Me
978-0-9562693-2-4

The 1st Comic Book
978-0-9562693-1-7

The 2nd Comic Book
978-0-95626934-8

The 3rd Comic Book
978-0-9562693-3-1

The 4th Comic Book
978-15086839-7-1

Websites:
www.alisrowe.co.uk
www.thegirlwiththecurlyhair.co.uk
www.womensweightlifting.co.uk

Social Media:
www.facebook.com/thegirlwiththecurlyhair
www.twitter.com/curlyhairedalis

The Visual Guide to

Asperger's Syndrome: Social Energy (1)

by Alis Rowe

Lonely Mind Books
London

For people with Asperger's Syndrome and their Neurotypical families and friends

hello

This is a subject close to my heart. Throughout my life, it is my social difficulties ('the triad of impairments') that have made me feel most stressed and unhappy. Add to the fact that I'm naturally a shy, quiet, introverted person, my social life has always been incredibly difficult.

From a young age, I was aware I had less capacity for social interactions than other people. This book is a collection of all my thoughts, ideas, findings about my experiences of socialising, in one place.

I hope you find it interesting, uplifting, empowering and, most of all, I hope you find it comforting.

Alis aka The Girl with the Curly Hair

Contents

WHAT IS ACTUALLY MEANT BY THE TERM 'AUTISM SPECTRUM DISORDER'?

"ASD IS A NEUROLOGICAL
CONDITION WHICH AFFECTS THE
WAY A PERSON COMMUNICATES AND
RELATES TO THE PEOPLE AND THE
WORLD AROUND THEM"

NATIONAL AUTISTIC SOCIETY

A PERSON WITH ASD HAS THREE PRIMARY CHALLENGES:

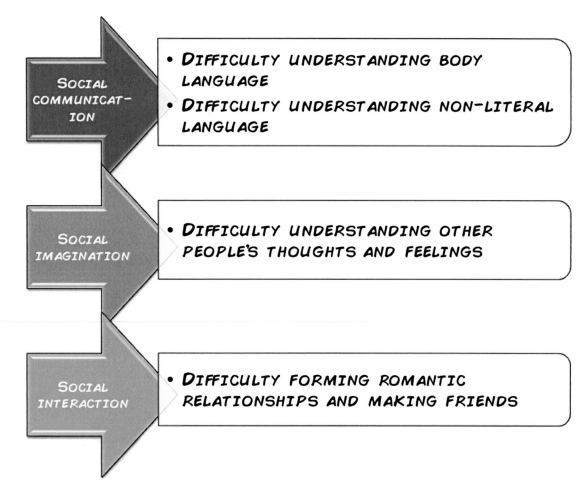

SOCIAL COMMUNICATION
- DIFFICULTY UNDERSTANDING BODY LANGUAGE
- DIFFICULTY UNDERSTANDING NON-LITERAL LANGUAGE

SOCIAL IMAGINATION
- DIFFICULTY UNDERSTANDING OTHER PEOPLE'S THOUGHTS AND FEELINGS

SOCIAL INTERACTION
- DIFFICULTY FORMING ROMANTIC RELATIONSHIPS AND MAKING FRIENDS

BECAUSE OF THEM, SOCIALISING MAY BE VERY DIFFICULT AND STRESSFUL

LET'S LOOK AT EACH ONE AND SEE
HOW THEY AFFECT THE GIRL WITH
THE CURLY HAIR'S ABILITY TO
SOCIALISE

What sort of social communication challenges does The Girl with the Curly Hair have?

How do I end a conversation without seeming rude?

I don't know how close to stand when I am talking to someone. I always worry I might be too close so I consciously make an effort to move further away

When is it my turn to speak? When is it their turn to speak? How long do I pause for?

I can't work out when somebody might be bored with what I am saying and when I should change the topic

What does it mean when they wink at me, or when they pat my back?

Why did they say they were only going to be "5 minutes"? It's been 11 minutes and they're still not back

Where do I look when I am speaking to someone? It feels awkward to keep looking in their eyes. It's hard having them look into mine

WHAT SORT OF SOCIAL IMAGINATION CHALLENGES DOES THE GIRL WITH THE CURLY HAIR HAVE?

WE ALWAYS HAVE SALMON ON MONDAYS. BUT TODAY IS MONDAY AND WE DON'T HAVE ANY SALMON IN THE FRIDGE. DOES THIS MEAN I WONT HAVE ANY DINNER TONIGHT?

I DON'T UNDERSTAND WHY MUM IS UPSET WITH ME. SHE IS SICK IN BED. I BROUGHT HER MEDICINE. WHAT MORE DOES SHE WANT ME TO DO?

MY FRIEND AND I HAVE ALWAYS CYCLED ROUND THE SAME PARK. NOW SHE WANTS TO CYCLE IN A DIFFERENT PARK. I DON'T WANT TO

WHY DOES MY PARTNER WANT ME TO KISS AND HUG HIM EVERY MORNING BEFORE HE GOES TO WORK? WHY DOES HE FEEL UNLOVED IF I DON'T DO IT?

MY FRIEND'S HUSBAND HAD AN AFFAIR AND SHE ASKED HIM TO LEAVE THE HOUSE AND GO AND LIVE SOMEWHERE ELSE. NOW SHE SAYS SHE FEELS ABANDONED. BUT SHE ASKED HIM TO LEAVE. I DON'T UNDERSTAND WHY SHE FEELS THIS WAY

I DON'T KNOW WHAT TO DO WHEN DAD SHOUTS AT ME AND SAYS "THE HOUSE IS A MESS." WHICH BIT IS A MESS? WHAT EXACTLY DOES HE WANT ME TO DO?

WHAT SORT OF SOCIAL INTERACTION CHALLENGES DOES THE GIRL WITH THE CURLY HAIR HAVE?

I FIND IT REALLY HARD TO TALK TO PEOPLE. MOST OF THE TIME, I JUST STAY ON OWN AND WILL ONLY SPEAK WHEN SPOKEN TO – AND EVEN THEN SOMETIMES I AM SILENT

I FEEL LIKE I CAN'T GO TO MY FRIEND'S BIRTHDAY PARTY BECAUSE IT'S AT THE 'WRONG' TIME WITH THE 'WRONG' FOOD

I DON'T FEEL LIKE I CAN BE MYSELF WHEN I AM IN PUBLIC. WHEN I MAKE AN EFFORT TO LOOK NICE, SMILE AND CHAT TO EVERYBODY ABOUT THE WEATHER AND WHAT'S ON THE T.V., I FEEL LIKE I AM NOT BEING ME

WHY DOES EVERYONE ELSE SEEM TO REALLY ENJOY PAIRING UP OR WORKING IN GROUPS? I JUST GET LEFT OUT

EVERYBODY ELSE HANGS OUT TOGETHER AT THE EVENINGS AND WEEKENDS. BUT I'M REALLY TIRED BY THEN AND NEED TO BE ON MY OWN. I FEEL DIFFERENT

LOTS OF PEOPLE GET EXCITED ABOUT GOING ON HOLIDAY OR GOING CLUBBING. I DON'T ENJOY THOSE THINGS. I FEEL DIFFERENT

I LIKE TO WEAR THE SAME CLOTHES EVERY DAY. I DON'T REALLY LIKE SHOWERING OR COMBING MY HAIR. I DON'T CARE ABOUT BRANDS OR LABELS AND I DON'T WEAR MAKEUP. I LOOK DIFFERENT

CONSEQUENTLY, SOCIALISING IS INCREDIBLY HARD WORK FOR PEOPLE WITH ASD

WHICH BRINGS US ON TO TALKING ABOUT 'ENERGY'...

WHAT IS ENERGY?

THE GIRL WITH THE CURLY HAIR THINKS OF ENERGY LIKE THIS:

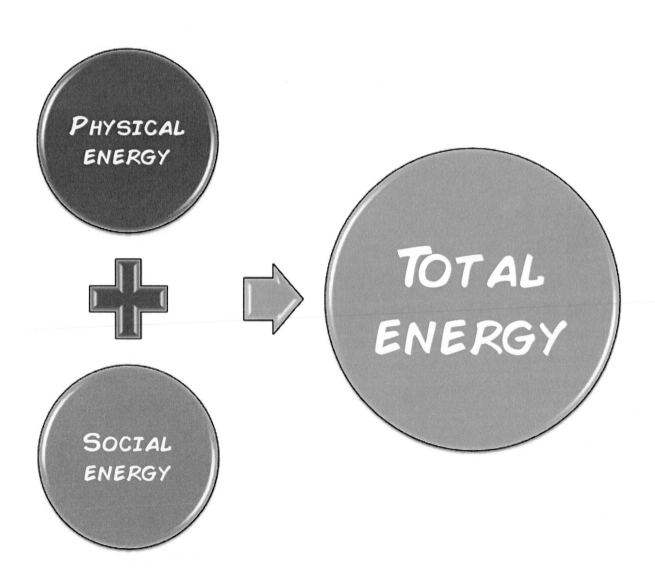

PHYSICAL ENERGY

PHYSICAL ENERGY IS MUCH EASIER FOR HER TO MANAGE

SHE EATS A HEALTHY, BALANCED DIET

SHE GETS HIGH QUALITY SLEEP EACH NIGHT

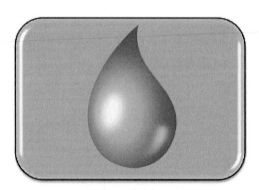

SHE KEEPS HYDRATED

SHE TAKES REGULAR EXERCISE

AS LONG AS SHE MAINTAINS THIS WAY OF LIVING, HER PHYSICAL ENERGY REMAINS HIGH...

SOCIAL ENERGY

SOCIAL ENERGY IS THE AMOUNT OF NON-PHYSICAL EFFORT REQUIRED FOR HER TO DO THE 'NORMAL' TASKS OF LIFE

THESE NORMAL TASKS CAN BE BIGGER THINGS...

GOING TO THE HAIR DRESSER'S	GOING ON HOLIDAY
A WORKOUT WITH A PERSONAL TRAINER	GOING TO THE SUPERMARKET
GOING TO THE BANK	MEETING UP WITH A FRIEND
SHOPPING FOR CLOTHES	GOING TO WORK

Or smaller things...

GETTING DRESSED IN THE MORNING	COOKING A MEAL
WALKING THE DOG	HAVING A SHOWER
TALKING ON THE TELEPHONE	ANSWERING THE FRONT DOOR
BUYING SOME BREAD AND MILK	CLEANING THE HOUSE

SOCIAL ENERGY IS, BASICALLY, THE EFFORT REQUIRED FOR *PRODUCTIVE* DAY TO DAY LIVING

IT IS WHAT'S NEEDED FOR THE GIRL WITH THE CURLY HAIR TO FUNCTION IN THE OUTSIDE, NEUROTYPICAL, WORLD...

THE GIRL WITH THE CURLY HAIR
FINDS SOCIALISING VERY TIRING

SHE SAYS HER SOCIAL ENERGY TANK IS SMALLER THAN THE SOCIAL ENERGY TANK OF HER NEUROTYPICAL COUNTERPART

THIS REPRESENTS THE NT EXTROVERT. THEY HAVE A LARGE TANK WHICH IS FULL TO THE BRIM

THIS REPRESENTS THE ASD EXTROVERT. THEY HAVE A SMALLER TANK THAN THE NT, BUT IT IS STILL FULL TO THE BRIM

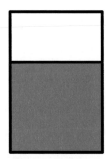

THIS REPRESENTS THE NT INTROVERT. THEY HAVE A LARGE TANK BUT IT IS NEVER ACTUALLY FULL

THIS REPRESENTS THE ASD INTROVERT. THEY HAVE A SMALLER TANK, WHICH IS NEVER FULL

CONSEQUENTLY, HER TANK EMPTIES MORE QUICKLY

SOME THINGS GIVE HER *MORE SOCIAL ENERGY*, SOME THINGS *CONSUME IT*, FOR EXAMPLE:

LOSSES	GAINS
• SOCIALISING	• SPECIAL INTERESTS
• SOCIAL INTERACTIONS	• HOBBIES
• CHANGES IN ROUTINE	• ALONE TIME
• TOO MUCH/THE 'WRONG' SENSORY INPUT	• EXERCISE/SLEEP/DIET
• EXECUTIVE FUNCTIONING/DAILY LIVING SKILLS	• ANIMALS AND NATURE
• FEELINGS OF ANXIETY	• MEDITATION
• RUMINATING	• ROUTINE
• POOR EXERCISE/SLEEP/DIET	

SHE TRIES TO MANAGE EACH DAY SO THAT HER SOCIAL ENERGY LASTS FOR THE WHOLE DAY AND SO THAT HER TANK NEVER ENDS UP COMPLETELY EMPTY...

THE AIM IS TO ENSURE THAT THE BALANCE BETWEEN THESE ENERGY-CONSUMING AND ENERGY-GAINING ACTIVITIES IS RIGHT DAY TO DAY

THIS MEANS UNDERSTANDING THAT SOME THINGS MAKE HER FEEL ENERGISED AND SOME THINGS MAKE HER FEEL DRAINED – AND THAT THINGS WILL AFFECT HER TO VARYING EXTENTS:

SOCIAL ENERGY GAIN OR LOSS

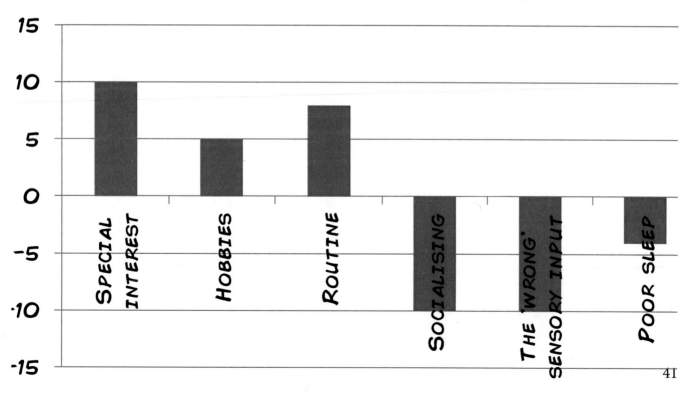

ON DIFFERENT DAYS, SHE HAS DIFFERENT CAPACITIES TO FACE THE WORLD. THIS MEANS HER SOCIAL ENERGY VALUES FOR ACTIVITIES MAY WELL CHANGE DAY TO DAY

SOME DAYS SHE MIGHT ONLY BE DRAINED -5 BY SOCIALISING AND NOT -10

THE HIGHER HER SOCIAL ENERGY IS *BEFORE* SHE DOES AN ACTIVITY, THE EASIER THE RECOVERY WILL BE, E.G. IF IT STARTS OUT AT 8 AND THE SOCIALISING DRAINS HER BY 5, SHE ENDS UP AT 3:

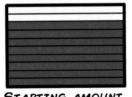
STARTING AMOUNT

AMOUNT GONE TO SOCIALISING

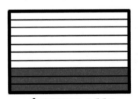
AMOUNT LEFT

AS OPPOSED TO IF SHE STARTS OUT AT 5 AND IS DRAINED BY 5, SHE ENDS UP AT ZERO:

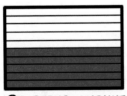
STARTING AMOUNT

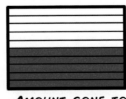
AMOUNT GONE TO SOCIALISING

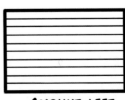
AMOUNT LEFT

WHAT HAPPENS WHEN HER SOCIAL ENERGY TANK BECOMES EMPTY?

SHE WILL HAVE EITHER A MELTDOWN

OR A SHUTDOWN

SOCIAL ENERGY IS USED UP ON DIFFERENT THINGS, SUCH AS...

THE SUPERMARKET...

SHE PUTS HER HOOD UP TO REDUCE ANXIETY AND INCREASE FEELINGS OF SECURITY AND PERSONAL SPACE

SHE AVOIDS THE BUSY TIMES AND GOES EARLY MORNING OR LATE AT NIGHT

SHE HAS THE CORRECT MONEY ON HER, TO REDUCE TIME SPENT INSIDE THE SHOP

SHE WEARS DARK SUNSHADES TO COMBAT THE BRIGHT LIGHTING

SHE ONLY USES THE SELF-SERVICE CHECKOUT, SO THAT SHE DOES NOT HAVE TO SPEAK TO ANYONE

SOMETIMES, SHE ONLY BUYS A SINGLE ITEM AT A TIME, PREFERRING TO MAKE MULTIPLE TRIPS AND SPEND LESS TIME INSIDE PER VISIT

SHE HAS A SHOPPING LIST SO KNOWS EXACTLY WHAT ITEMS SHE NEEDS AND WHERE SHE'LL BE ABLE TO FIND THEM

SHE WEARS EAR PLUGS TO DAMPEN THE SOUND

SHE NEVER SHOPS THE FEW DAYS BEFORE CHRISTMAS. SHE GOES IN ADVANCE

THE OFFICE...

EVEN IF SHE'S HAVING A BAD DAY, SHE FEELS SHE HAS TO REMAIN PERSONABLE AND PLEASANT TO HER COLLEAGUES, BUT IT'S EXHAUSTING

SHE FINDS IT HARD TO PROCESS CONVERSATION WITH COLLEAGUES AT THE SAME TIME AS COPING WITH THE SOUND OF THE PHOTOCOPIER AND THE FLICKERING LIGHTS

SHE DOESN'T FEEL THE NEED TO SPEAK UNLESS THERE IS SOMETHING TO SAY. LISTENING TO OTHER PEOPLE'S 'ADDITIONAL' WORDS IS CONFUSING

SHE GETS VERY FOCUSSED ON THE WORK SHE IS DOING. IT IS VERY DISRUPTIVE WHEN SOMEONE TRIES TO TALK TO HER WHEN SHE IS WORKING

HER EARS ARE SO SENSITIVE THAT SOCIAL CHAT IN THE OFFICE IS VERY DISTRACTING

PEOPLE ARE TALKING ALL THE TIME, EVEN IF NOT TALKING TO HER. IT TAKES A LOT OF EFFORT TO IGNORE THEM

SHE DOES NOT LIKE IT WHEN PEOPLE EAT BANANAS AND DRINK COFFEE IN THE OFFICE. IT MAKES HER FEEL SICK

SHE HAS TO REMEMBER TO SAY "HI, HOW ARE YOU?" EVERY DAY AND "HOW WAS YOUR WEEKEND?" EVERY MONDAY MORNING. THEN SHE HAS TO CARRY ON THE CONVERSATION A LITTLE SO AS NOT TO APPEAR RUDE

SHE WANTS TO FIDGET AND SPIN ON HER CHAIR BUT SHE HAS TO RESTRAIN HERSELF BECAUSE IT WILL SEEM ODD

SHE HAS TO WORK OUT WHAT OTHER PEOPLE'S GESTURES AND EXPRESSIONS MEAN

SCHOOL...

She would like the lesson to start and finish exactly on time. It especially upsets her when the class starts later than it's supposed to

She prefers to be given step-by-step written instructions (as opposed to verbal) for all assignments

She does not want to be 'picked on' for being quiet or continuously asked to speak up. Her self-esteem is low already

It would be helpful if the teacher wrote a list of lesson's goals on the whiteboard, before the class begins

She would prefer the windows to be closed in order to reduce outside noise in the playground or on the road, which is very distracting

She would like the teacher to fix that flickering light above her head. It is very distracting

She does not want to be unexpectedly chosen to stand at the front of the class to write or draw something on the whiteboard. This is very anxiety-provoking

She finds eye contact hard. But just because she is not looking at the teacher, it does not mean she isn't listening. She is in fact, listening very hard!

She cannot write notes and listen to the teacher speak simultaneously. She prefers just to write the notes

She is extremely uncomfortable working in groups and prefers to work alone. If it is imperative for her to work in a group, she would like the teacher to assign pupils to groups, rather than let them pick their own (she always gets left out)

WITH FRIENDS...

SHE WON'T EAT LUNCH WITH THEM BECAUSE SHE'S SO FUSSY ABOUT HER OWN DIET AND TIME SCHEDULE. SHE HAS TO EAT AT HOME AND SHE HAS TO EAT WHAT SHE HAS PLANNED TO EAT WHEN SHE HAS PLANNED IT

SOMETIMES SHE MAKES THE EFFORT TO GO OUT WITH THEM BUT MOST SOCIAL ENVIRONMENTS ARE TOO SENSORY STIMULATING

SHE PREFERS TO CONVERSE WITH HER FRIENDS THROUGH SOCIAL MEDIA AND TEXT MESSAGING, WHEREAS MOST OF THEM PREFER TO MEET UP IN PERSON

SHE ALWAYS FEELS AN OBSERVER IN HER GROUP OF FRIENDS, RATHER THAN A PART OF IT

SHE HAS TO FIT SEEING HER FRIENDS AROUND HER RIGID ROUTINE, OTHERWISE SHE GETS STRESSED AND ANXIOUS

SHE LOVES HER FRIENDS BUT IS AWARE THAT THEY ENJOY DIFFERENT THINGS FROM HER...

SHE FINDS IT HARD SPENDING LONG PERIODS OF TIME WITH HER FRIENDS. ONE HOUR IS ENOUGH

...AND WISHES SOMETIMES THAT SHE ENJOYED THE SAME THINGS AS THEM

SHE SPENDS SO MUCH SOCIAL ENERGY AT WORK, THAT SHE DOESN'T HAVE MUCH LEFT TO SEE HER FRIENDS AT THE WEEKENDS OR IN THE EVENINGS...

...AND ALWAYS FEELS GUILTY THAT SHE MIGHT HURT THEM BY NOT SEEING THEM VERY OFTEN

WHEREAS NTS CAN JUST PLAN TO GET THE TRAIN, SHE DWELLS ON THE PLAN TO GET THE TRAIN...

FIND OUT TRAIN DEPARTURE TIME MAKE SURE TO KNOW WHEN THE NEXT TRAIN IS, IN CASE THERE IS A CANCELLATION

MAKE SURE HAVE ENOUGH MONEY FOR TICKET MAKE SURE TICKET OFFICE IS OPEN

AVOID CROWDS DECIDE WHICH CARRIAGE IS LIKELY TO BE THE LEAST CROWDED

GET ON TRAIN

THE GIRL WITH THE CURLY HAIR FINDS IT HARD TO MAINTAIN A FULL TIME JOB

BECAUSE THE SOCIAL ENERGY NEEDED AT WORK, IN ORDER FOR HER TO CARRY OUT HER JOB, LEAVES HER WITH NO MORE IN THE TANK FOR FAMILY AND FRIENDS (THE PEOPLE WHO MATTER TO HER MOST)

SPENDING ALL THAT TIME AROUND PEOPLE DURING THE WEEK MEANS SHE JUST WANTS TO BE ON HER OWN AT WEEKENDS

MONDAY	
TUESDAY	
WEDNESDAY	
THURSDAY	
FRIDAY	
SATURDAY	
SUNDAY	

After work, she needs to be on her own too

TIME	ACTIVITY
BEFORE WORK	ALONE TIME
9AM	START WORK
10AM	BREAK ALONE
11AM	WORK
12PM	LUNCH ALONE
1PM	WORK
2PM	WORK
3PM	BREAK ALONE
4PM	WORK
5PM	FINISH WORK
AFTER WORK	ALONE TIME

By the time she gets home from work, she has very little social energy left

NO MORE AVAILABLE FOR SOCIALISING IN THE PUB AFTER WORK OR GOING OUT TO A RESTAURANT FOR DINNER

So, in the evenings, when she seems a bit withdrawn, it's not a personal attack on anyone

She's just looking after herself and regenerating some of that precious social energy

BEING ALONE AT WEEKENDS MEANS SHE CAN REGENERATE THE SOCIAL ENERGY THAT'S BEEN LOST DURING THE WORKING WEEK...

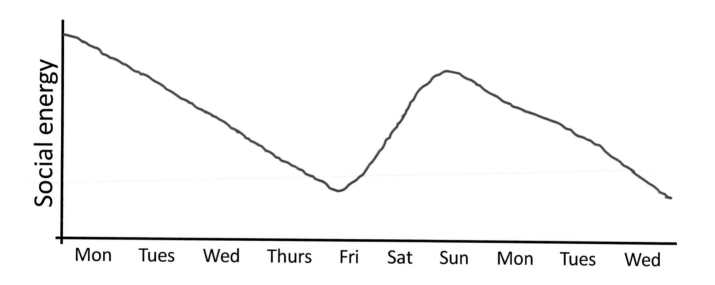

...JUST IN TIME FOR THE FOLLOWING MONDAY

THE NEUROTYPICAL WORLD IS VERY SOCIAL

SHE IS EXPECTED TO BE POLITE, PERSONABLE AND PLEASANT AT ALL TIMES

SMALL TALK AND GENERAL CHIT CHAT USE UP A LOT OF SOCIAL ENERGY

SHE DESCRIBES THIS EXPERIENCE OF THE NEUROTYPICAL WORLD USING 'HOT POTATO THEORY':

(BLUE REPRESENTS THE GIRL WITH THE CURLY HAIR'S PERCEIVED 'UNCOMFORTABLE SILENCE'

'CHATTER' GETS PASSED FROM ONE PERSON TO THE OTHER IN A WAY WHICH FEELS LIKE A HOT POTATO...)

Hot Potato Theory explains the feeling that there's always an expectation to speak, even when she doesn't want to

This can happen anywhere – the bus stop, the doctor's waiting room, outside the classroom, walking the dog, etc....

IF SHE HAS NO SOCIAL ENERGY LEFT WHEN SHE IS AT HOME, AWAY FROM THE NEUROTYPICAL OUTSIDE WORLD, SHE TENDS TO BE QUIET, WITHDRAWN AND ALOOF

CONSEQUENTLY, HER RELATIONSHIPS WITH FRIENDS AND FAMILY SUFFER

THEY ALWAYS WITNESS HER IN A 'FATIGUED' STATE

THE MANAGEMENT AND MAINTENANCE
OF RELATIONSHIPS IS DIFFICULT

SHE CAN SOCIALISE WITH SOMEONE FOR AN HOUR OR TWO BUT THEN SHE'LL NEVER CALL THE PERSON BACK OR SEE THEM AGAIN

JUST BECAUSE SHE DOESN'T HAVE THE SOCIAL ENERGY TO MAKE THE PHONE CALL! MAKING THE EFFORT TO KEEP IN TOUCH IS HARD

THIS IS THE PROCESS SHE HAS TO GO THROUGH EVERY TIME SHE ATTENDS A A SOCIAL EVENT:

SHE SPENDS THE WHOLE WEEK MENTALLY PREPARING FOR THE PARTY

The week before

The hours before

SHE SPENDS THE DAY RESEARCHING CURRENT AFFAIRS OR THE LATEST FILMS SO THAT SHE HAS THINGS TO TALK ABOUT

At the end of the party

BEFORE SHE GOES HOME, THEY ASK FOR HER NUMBER AND EMAIL ADDRESS. THEY ASK HER WHETHER SHE CAN HELP ON A WEBSITE, OR TELL HER WHY SHE SHOULD JOIN THE LOCAL IT SOCIETY

SOME PEOPLE TALK TO HER AND FIND OUT SHE'S REALLY GOOD AT COMPUTERS

During the party

SHE GOES HOME. SHE FEELS EXHAUSTED. SHE MADE AN EFFORT TO GO THE PARTY. SHE WAS NICE. SHE WAS PLEASANT. BUT SHE GOES HOME FEELING OVERWHELMED, BECAUSE IT FEELS LIKE THEY JUST ALWAYS WANT MORE

The hours after

SHE SWITCHES HER PHONE OFF AND SHUTS HERSELF AWAY IN HER HOME IN ORDER TO RECOVER

The days after

It's hard feeling lonely and wanting to be with people but not being able to connect with them in the same way they connect with each other

This is known as 'The Dissociation Effect'

'The Dissociation Effect'

The Girl with the Curly Hair thinks that, during socialising, people with ASD 'dissociate' whereas neurotypicals 'associate'

She also thinks that neurotypicals tend to start off feeling "closer" (or more "connected") than people with ASD...

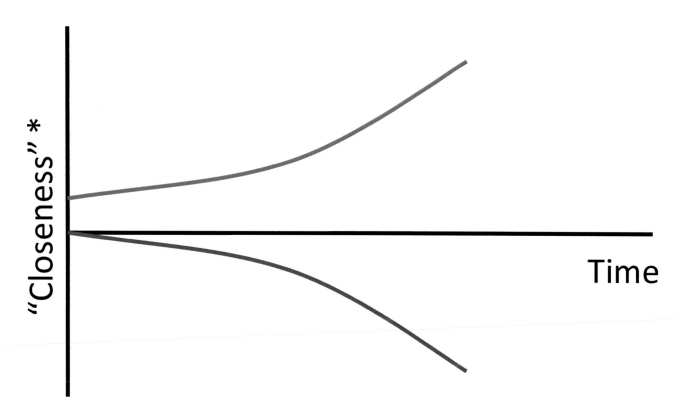

*"CLOSENESS" MAY BE DEFINED AS THE INITIAL FEELING OF CONNECTION OR SAME WAVELENGTH THAT HUMAN BEINGS EXPERIENCE UPON FIRST MEETING ONE ANOTHER

DURING PERIODS OF SOCIALISING, THE GIRL WITH THE CURLY HAIR OFTEN EXPERIENCES 'DISSOCIATION':

AT THE START:

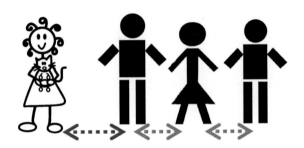

IN THE MIDDLE:

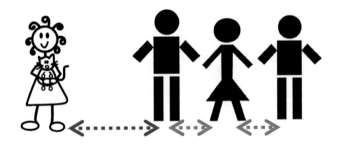

AT THE END:

IT ALSO SEEMS LIKE EVERYONE ELSE IS EXPERIENCING 'ASSOCIATION' AT THE SAME RATE THAT SHE IS EXPERIENCING DISSOCIATION, WHICH REINFORCES HOW LONELY SHE ENDS UP FEELING

WHAT HAPPENS THEREFORE, WHEN THE GIRL WITH THE CURLY HAIR GOES TO A PARTY?

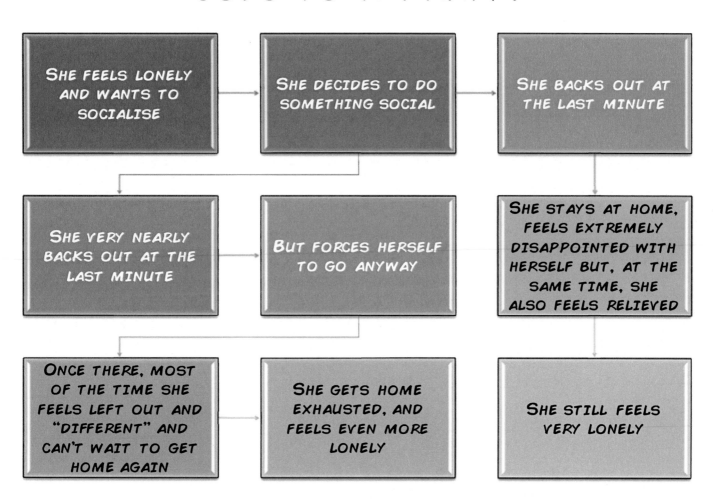

SHE FEELS LONELY AND WANTS TO SOCIALISE

SHE DECIDES TO DO SOMETHING SOCIAL

SHE BACKS OUT AT THE LAST MINUTE

SHE VERY NEARLY BACKS OUT AT THE LAST MINUTE

BUT FORCES HERSELF TO GO ANYWAY

SHE STAYS AT HOME, FEELS EXTREMELY DISAPPOINTED WITH HERSELF BUT, AT THE SAME TIME, SHE ALSO FEELS RELIEVED

ONCE THERE, MOST OF THE TIME SHE FEELS LEFT OUT AND "DIFFERENT" AND CAN'T WAIT TO GET HOME AGAIN

SHE GETS HOME EXHAUSTED, AND FEELS EVEN MORE LONELY

SHE STILL FEELS VERY LONELY

It's very hard going through day to day life with a smaller social energy tank than everybody else

OVER TIME SHE HAS DEVELOPED HER OWN COPING STRATEGIES, SUCH AS:

KEEPING DAILY ACTIVITIES TO A MINIMUM

HAVING A QUIET DAY IF THE DAY BEFORE HAS BEEN A BUSY ONE

SAYING "NO" TO THINGS MORE OFTEN

BEING ALONE IN THE EVENINGS

CHOOSING TO DO THINGS, RATHER THAN BEING PRESSURED TO DO THINGS

LEAVING SOCIAL EVENTS EARLY

SPENDING MORE TIME ON HER OWN OR WITH LOVED ONES AND LESS TIME WITH COLLEAGUES AND CLASSMATES

IF SHE HAS AN EMPTY DAY, SHE HAS CAREFULLY PLANNED IT SO THAT SHE HAS THE TIME TO REGENERATE HER SOCIAL ENERGY

IT DOES NOT MEAN THAT SHE IS AVAILABLE FOR SOCIALISING!

REAL FRIENDS UNDERSTAND THAT'S JUST HOW SHE IS AND DON'T TAKE PERSONALLY HER LACK OF CONTACT OR THE AMOUNT OF TIME THEY SPEND APART

How do The Girl with the Curly Hair's friends help her manage her social energy?

Her friends are happy to make the first move to contact her to see how she's doing or what she's up to

They understand how important her routine is and are flexible themselves to fit in with her

They invite her to their birthday, Christmas, house warming parties, etc. and they don't mind if she doesn't make it

They meet up with each other in quiet, familiar places where she feels most comfortable and least anxious

They think of her first when they need advice on the things she is interested in, such as exercise and computers. It's a good way for them to bond

They don't ever expect to see her in the evenings. In fact, some of them really enjoy very early morning chats instead!

They enjoy texting and emailing each other more than speaking on the phone

They enjoy coming over to her house

They understand if she cancels last minute, as long as she lets them know

AND THOSE ARE THE PEOPLE WITH WHOM SHE DOES NOT SUFFER SOCIAL ANXIETY OR, IF SHE DOES, IT'S VERY LITTLE

SHE LOVES HER FRIENDS AND TRIES
HARD TO MAKE SURE THEY KNOW
HOW MUCH SHE APPRECIATES THEM

EVEN IF HER WAYS ARE LESS
CONVENTIONAL

INTROVERSION AND EXTROVERSION IN ASD

THE SOCIAL ENERGY TANKS ARE A USEFUL WAY TO THINK ABOUT EXTROVERTED AND INTROVERTED INDIVIDUALS:

THIS REPRESENTS THE NT EXTROVERT. THEY HAVE A LARGE TANK WHICH IS FULL TO THE BRIM

THIS REPRESENTS THE ASD EXTROVERT. THEY HAVE A SMALLER TANK THAN THE NT, BUT IT IS STILL FULL TO THE BRIM

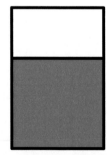

THIS REPRESENTS THE NT INTROVERT. THEY HAVE A LARGE TANK BUT IT IS NEVER ACTUALLY FULL

THIS REPRESENTS THE ASD INTROVERT. THEY HAVE A SMALLER TANK, WHICH IS NEVER FULL

What happens to social energy levels before and during socialising?

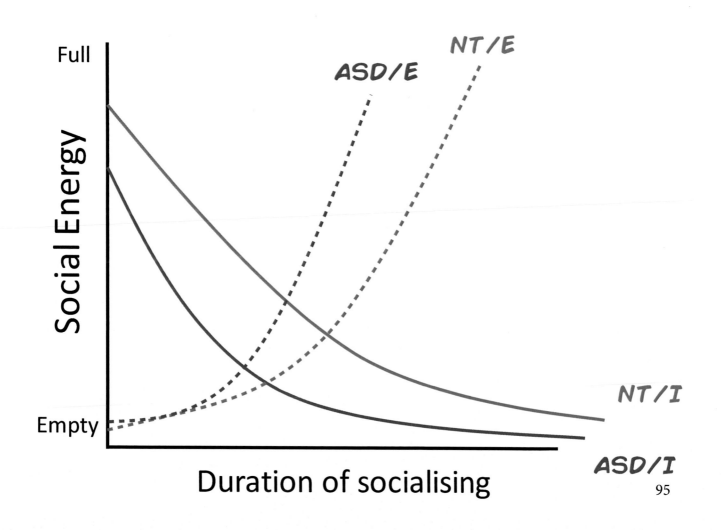

IF WE LOOK AT THESE IN MORE DETAIL...

THE ASD INTROVERT:

NEVER HAS A FULL SOCIAL
ENERGY TANK TO START
WITH (THEREFORE HAS LESS
DESIRE AND CAPACITY FOR
SOCIALISING ANYWAY)

LOSES SOCIAL ENERGY
DURING SOCIALISING

LOSES SOCIAL ENERGY AT
A FASTER RATE THAN THE
NT INTROVERT (BECAUSE
THE TANK IS SMALLER)

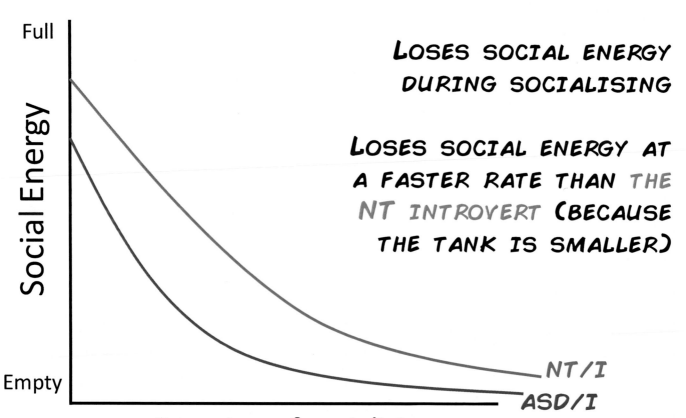

THE ASD EXTROVERT:

NEEDS SOCIAL INTERACTION TO GAIN SOCIAL ENERGY

REACHES MAXIMUM CAPACITY FOR SOCIAL INTERACTION FASTER THAN THE NT EXTROVERT AND HAS LESS CAPACITY FOR SOCIAL INTERACTION THAN THE NT EXTROVERT (BECAUSE THE TANK IS SMALLER)

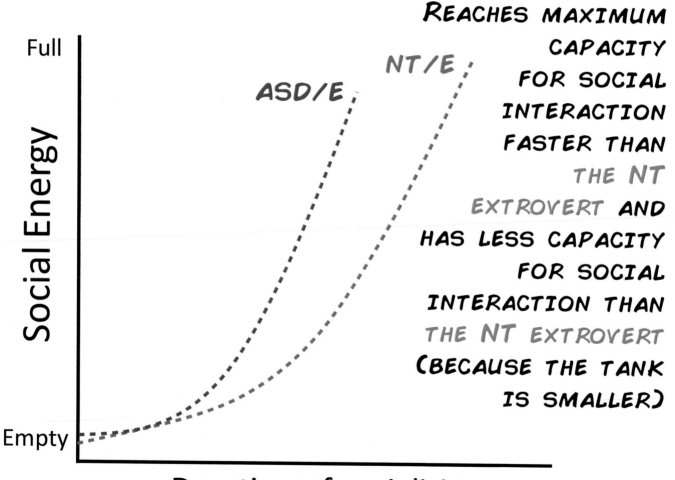

Full

Social Energy

Empty

ASD/E

NT/E

Duration of socialising

IT IS USUALLY ASSUMED THAT PEOPLE WITH ASD ARE INTROVERTED. WHY?

PEOPLE WITH ASD HAVE A TENDENCY TO...

- BE LONERS
- PREFER SOLITARY ACTIVITIES RATHER THAN SOCIAL ONES
- BE INDEPENDENT WORKERS RATHER THAN TEAM PLAYERS
- HAVE OBSESSIONS WITH CERTAIN THINGS AND DEVOTE THEIR TIME TO THESE THINGS, RATHER THAN TO PEOPLE
- LACK EMPATHY AND THEORY OF MIND
- FIND IT INCREDIBLY HARD TO BUILD CONNECTIONS AND FRIENDSHIPS
- SUFFER SOCIAL ANXIETY
- VERY EASILY FEEL OVERWHELMED BY PEOPLE AND NORMAL DAY TO DAY ACTIVITIES
- NEED TIME ALONE TO RECOVER FROM DAY TO DAY ACTIVITIES

BUT THE GIRL WITH THE CURLY HAIR KNOWS THIS ISN'T ACTUALLY THE CASE

REMEMBER WE TALKED ABOUT THE THREE PRIMARY CHALLENGES?

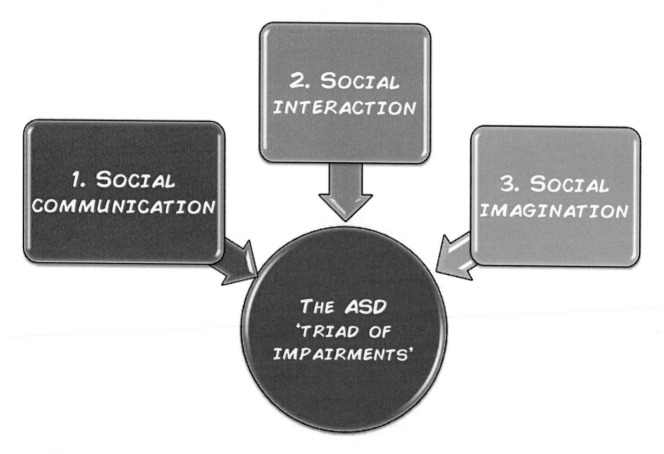

2. SOCIAL INTERACTION

1. SOCIAL COMMUNICATION

3. SOCIAL IMAGINATION

THE ASD 'TRIAD OF IMPAIRMENTS'

EVERYONE WITH ASD HAS THEM, REGARDLESS OF WHETHER THEY ARE INTROVERTED OR EXTROVERTED

WHAT ARE SOME CHALLENGES OF THE ASD INTROVERT AND THE ASD EXTROVERT?

THE ASD INTROVERT

- WANTS TO BE ON HER OWN AND MAY COME ACROSS AS WITHDRAWN OR ALOOF
- IS WELL LIKED
- FEELS FRUSTRATED SHE HAS A FRIEND AND IS A FRIEND, YET CAN'T QUITE MANAGE IT IN THE SAME WAY OTHERS CAN

THE ASD EXTROVERT

- WANTS TO BE AROUND PEOPLE BUT COMES ACROSS WRONG OR SOCIALLY INAPPROPRIATELY
- MAKES THE PEOPLE AROUND THEM FEEL STRESSED OR UNCOMFORTABLE
- FEELS FRUSTRATED THAT SHE WANTS SO DESPERATELY TO HAVE A FRIEND AND BE A FRIEND YET IT NEVER SEEMS TO WORK

THE GIRL WITH THE CURLY HAIR IS AN INTROVERT BUT WONDERS WHAT IT'S LIKE TO BE AN EXTROVERT...

SHE WONDERS WHETHER IT MIGHT BE *MORE DIFFICULT BEING AN EXTROVERT WITH ASD?*

INTROVERT
I DON'T HAVE MANY FRIENDS BUT I PREFER MY OWN COMPANY
PEOPLE USUALLY JUST THINK I'M NATURALLY QUIET OR VERY SHY
I FIND SOCIALISING HARD WORK AND EXHAUSTING. I CAN TAKE IT OR LEAVE IT
I FEEL ENERGISED BEING MY BY MYSELF

WHAT MIGHT AN EXTROVERT WITH ASD BE LIKE?

THEY'RE NOT TOO SHY TO SAY "HI" TO STRANGERS. THEY SMILE, EVEN AT PEOPLE THEY DON'T KNOW

THEY HAVE NO SOCIAL BOUNDARIES

THEIR LIFE MIGHT BE DESCRIBED AS LOUD AND "CHILDISH", WITH BIG EMOTIONS AND BIG MOOD SWINGS, EVEN WHEN IN PUBLIC

THEY MIGHT NOT GET THE OPPORTUNITY TO GO TO PARTIES AND SOCIAL GATHERINGS OFTEN, BUT, WHEN THEY DO, THEY REALLY ENJOY THEM

THEY TEND TO BE VERY LOUD BUT WON'T NECESSARILY REALISE

PARTICULARLY IF A GROUP ASSIGNMENT IS ABOUT THEIR SPECIAL INTEREST, THEY LOVE TO TAKE THE LEAD ROLE

THEY WILL JUMP IN IMMEDIATELY TO ANY SOCIAL SITUATION REGARDING THEIR SPECIAL INTEREST

THEY TALK MORE THAN LISTEN AND TEND TO INTERRUPT OTHERS WHEN THEY ARE SPEAKING

THEY LOVE PEOPLE AND DESPERATELY CRAVE INTERACTION BUT LACK REAL FRIENDSHIPS

THEY LOVE TALKING BUT OFTEN MISS THE SOCIAL SIGNALS AND TEND TO TALK TOO MUCH

THEY ARE OFTEN DESCRIBED AS BEING VERY OPENLY "ECCENTRIC", "WEIRD", "OFFENSIVE" OR "ANNOYING"

'THE INVADER/ INVADED' THEORY

AN INTROVERT WITH ASD HAS A VERY BIG PERSONAL SPACE, WHEREAS AN EXTROVERT WITH ASD HAS A VERY SMALL PERSONAL SPACE:

BECAUSE THE INTROVERT'S SPACE
IS SO BIG, SHE ALWAYS FEELS
SOMEBODY ELSE* IS PUSHING
INTO IT. SHE IS KNOWN AS 'THE
INVADED'...

BECAUSE THE EXTROVERT'S SPACE
IS SO SMALL, SHE ALWAYS FINDS
HERSELF INSIDE SOMEBODY ELSE'S.
SHE IS KNOWN AS 'THE INVADER'...

*IN THESE EXAMPLES, THE NT HAS AN 'AVERAGE'
AMOUNT OF PERSONAL SPACE

THIS EXPLAINS WHY *THE GIRL WITH THE CURLY HAIR* – AN *ASD* INTROVERT – ALWAYS FEELS OVERWHELMED

A LINE OF FOUR NEUROTYPICAL PEOPLE CAN FEEL FINE IN EACH OTHER'S COMPANY (THEIR PERSONAL SPACES DON'T OVERLAP)...

BUT IF WE REPLACE ONE NEUROTYPICAL WITH A PERSON WITH ASD, THEY ARE LIKELY TO FEEL OVERWHELMED (LOOK AT HOW THE SPACES ARE OVERLAPPING)...

THE GIRL WITH THE CURLY HAIR BELIEVES IN SOMETHING CALLED 'SOCIAL GEAR THEORY':

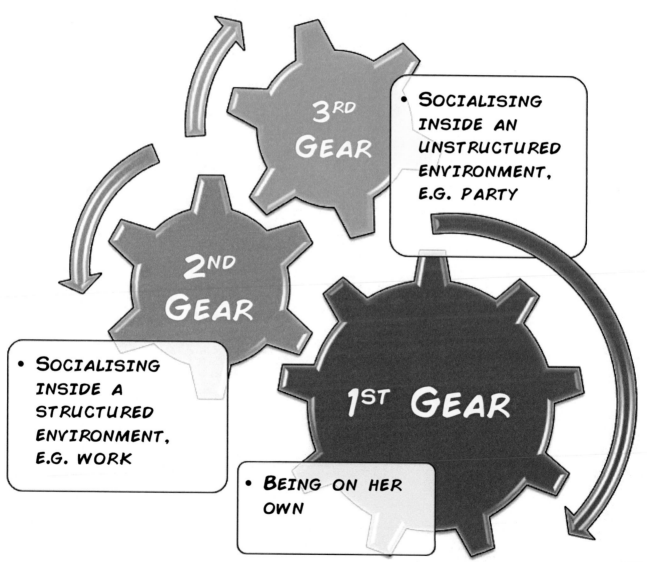

SOCIAL GEAR THEORY PROPOSES
TWO THINGS:

1. SOCIALISING IN UNSTRUCTURED
SITUATIONS IS DIFFICULT

2. SOCIALISING WITH THE
SAME PEOPLE IN DIFFERENT
ENVIRONMENTS IS DIFFICULT

WHEREAS NTs HAVE SEVERAL GEARS
WHICH THEY ARE ABLE TO FLIP
BETWEEN

THE GIRL WITH THE CURLY HAIR
OFTEN FEELS LIKE SHE'S MISSING
SOME GEARS

OR, SOMETIMES, IT FEELS LIKE SHE
SIMPLY GETS STUCK IN 1ST GEAR

GENERALLY, THE MORE UNSTRUCTURED THE SOCIAL SETTING, THE HARDER IT IS TO SOCIALISE, E.G....

Difficulty ↑

A PARTY
A PUB

WORK/SCHOOL
BOOK CLUB

Socialising with People 'Outside of Context' is Tricky:

With people at work	With the same people in the pub after work
• She can talk about work • They all have the same overall objective – to do good work for their company and to earn a living	• She feels she can't talk about work • She sits in silence whilst everyone else seems able to change their "social gear". They feel relaxed talking about other things

Due to social imagination difficulties and rigid thinking, The Girl with the Curly Hair prefers to keep the people around her very separate, e.g. in this diagram:

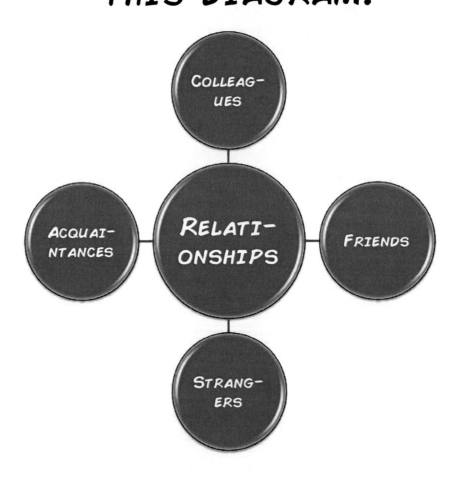

COMPARED TO THIS DIAGRAM, WHERE THE PEOPLE ARE IN MORE THAN ONE CIRCLE AND CAN MOVE AROUND:

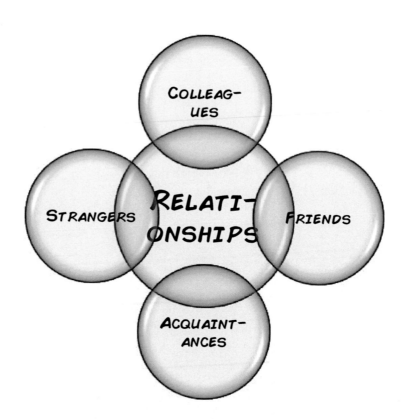

Over time, The Girl with the Curly Hair has developed her own strategies to make socialising a bit easier...

LIKE FINDING AND FOCUSING ON JUST ONE THING SHE LIKES ABOUT A PERSON. THIS IS USUALLY SOMETHING SHE ADMIRES OR FINDS AMUSING...

NEIGHBOUR JOHN, THE STOIC SON WITH A DISABLED MOTHER

Admiration

RACHEL, A PEER, WHO PLAYS TRICKS ON ALL THE TEACHERS

Amusement

DANIEL, WHO SITS OPPOSITE HER, GOES TO THE GYM EVERY DAY

Admiration

SHE CAN COPE WITH PEOPLE BY APPRECIATING THE ONE COOL, UNIQUE THING ABOUT THEM AND SHOWING THEM THAT THIS ONE THING IS SPECIAL AND VALUABLE!

IF SHE WANTS TO TALK ABOUT HER SPECIAL INTEREST (WEIGHTLIFTING) BUT ISN'T SURE HOW TO, SHE FOLLOWS THIS GUIDE...

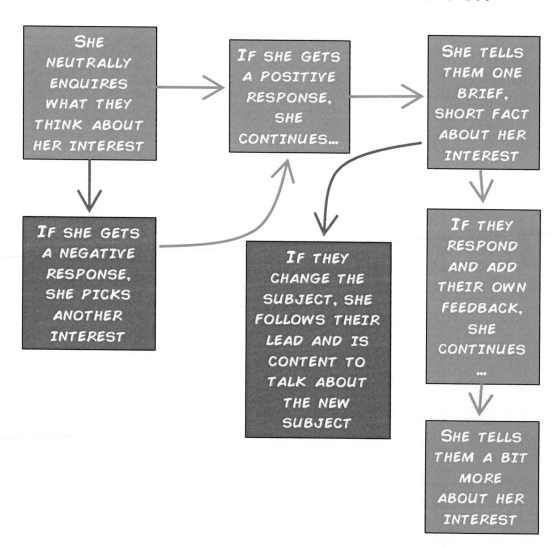

SHE NEUTRALLY ENQUIRES WHAT THEY THINK ABOUT HER INTEREST

IF SHE GETS A POSITIVE RESPONSE, SHE CONTINUES...

SHE TELLS THEM ONE BRIEF, SHORT FACT ABOUT HER INTEREST

IF SHE GETS A NEGATIVE RESPONSE, SHE PICKS ANOTHER INTEREST

IF THEY CHANGE THE SUBJECT, SHE FOLLOWS THEIR LEAD AND IS CONTENT TO TALK ABOUT THE NEW SUBJECT

IF THEY RESPOND AND ADD THEIR OWN FEEDBACK, SHE CONTINUES ...

SHE TELLS THEM A BIT MORE ABOUT HER INTEREST

SHE HAS WORKED OUT A WAY TO
KNOW WHEN IT'S TIME TO SAY
"HELLO"...

1. WHEN SHE SPOTS SOMEONE IN THE NEAR DISTANCE, SHE RAISES HER HEAD AND MAKES THE INITIAL EYE CONTACT

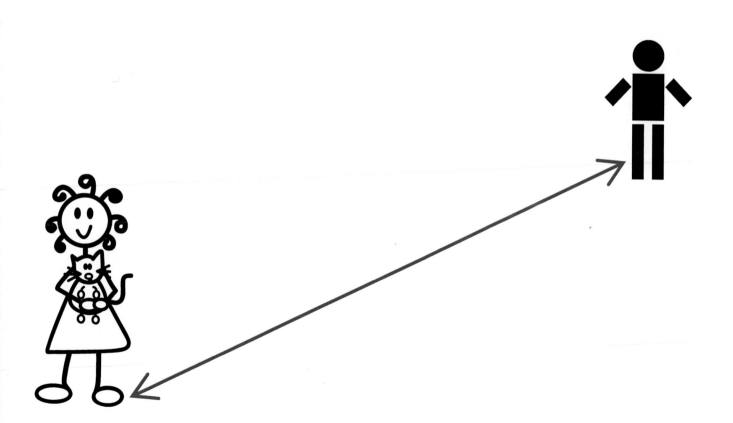

2. Then she looks down again and continues walking, getting nearer and nearer to them

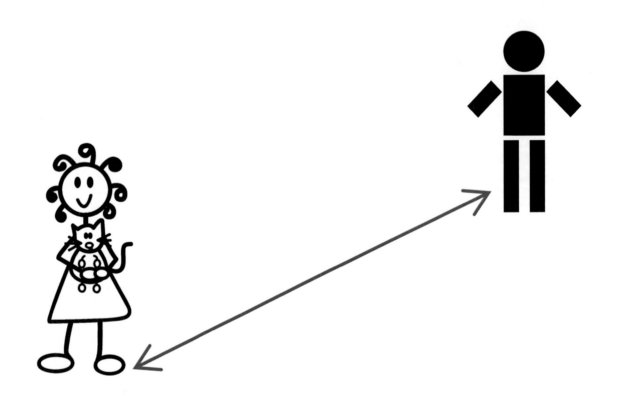

3. When they are about 2 metres apart she lifts her head and says "hello"

4. THEN, REGARDLESS OF WHETHER OR NOT THEY SAY "HELLO" BACK, SHE CONTINUES ON HER WAY (JOB DONE!)

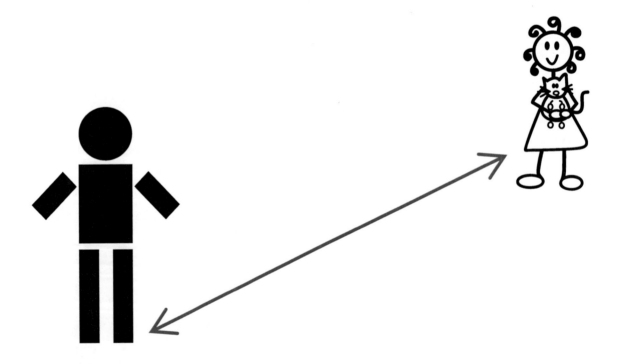

The Girl with the Curly Hair has 3 tips to help her have conversations with others...

1. Be aware of the 'direct' ASD personality type and never <u>force</u> your presence on others

2. Allow <u>time</u> for the other person to speak. It's helpful to let them initiate or continue the dialogue

3. Keep your eye on the "<u>big picture.</u>" Be aware of outside factors, such as the other person's mood, their stress or distraction levels etc., that can also determine how well a conversation will go

As you can imagine, having to learn the strategies, which are intuitive to others, is hard work and very tiring for people with ASD

OFTEN, *THE GIRL WITH THE CURLY HAIR* FEELS LIKE SHE LIVES INSIDE A GLASS JAR

ALWAYS OBSERVING, NEVER REALLY PARTICIPATING. WHENEVER SHE TRIES TO CONNECT WITH ANYONE, THERE IS ALWAYS A GLASS WALL IN THE WAY

NOT BEING ABLE TO INTUITIVELY CONNECT WITH OTHERS LEAVES THE PERSON WITH ASD FEELING VERY DISCONNECTED FROM THE WORLD

WHEREAS A SHY *NEUROTYPICAL PERSON* CAN BE 'PULLED OUT OF THEIR SHELL', A PERSON WITH **ASD** CANNOT BE PULLED OUT OF THEIR GLASS JAR:

THE PERSON WITH **ASD** *HAS TO COME OUT IN THEIR OWN WAY, IN THEIR OWN TIME.* 'FORCING' SOMEONE OUT BEFORE THEY ARE READY COULD LEAD TO A MELTDOWN

IS IT ANY WONDER THAT PEOPLE WITH ASD HAVE LESS SOCIAL ENERGY THAN NEUROTYPICAL PEOPLE?

As their loved one, how can you help a person with ASD cope in social situations?

Meet one another in reduced sensory-stimulating environments so that they can focus on you and your conversation rather than the light, sound, smell, etc.

Include them in the things you do so always invite them to join in with whatever you are doing...

...But if they say "no", respect their decision but let them know it's OK to change their mind. Do not, however, put any pressure on them

In big groups, they often feel left out. Help them to befriend each member of the group individually

Talk to them about their interests. They will usually be delighted that someone wants to know about it and gives them a chance to raise their confidence

Be accommodating and try to fit in with their routine – or at least be respectful of it. If they can't meet you because it's the 'wrong' time, understand that this is important to them and perhaps ask them what would be the 'right' time?

Learn the signs of being overwhelmed and, if you sense they are starting to experience it, suggest a way to end the situation

BE SENSITIVE TO ANY BEHAVIOUR THAT MIGHT APPEAR A BIT UNUSUAL OR ODD...

HAND FLAPPING	TALKING TOO LOUD	TALKING TOO MUCH
NOT TALKING AT ALL	STANDING TOO CLOSE	NOT MAKING EYE CONTACT
SMILING/LAUGHING AT THE 'WRONG' THING	EXPRESSING BLUNT OR BRUTAL HONESTY	HAVING AN ODD POSTURE OR GAIT
ENDING A CONVERSATION WITHOUT SAYING GOODBYE	UNUSUAL HAND GESTURES	ALWAYS WEARING THE SAME CLOTHES OR HAVING A QUIRKY DRESS SENSE

How can the person with ASD manage their own social energy better?

Do less

- Say "no" more often
- Prioritise

Avoid triggers

- Being out of routine, disrupted sleep, social events

Manage triggers

- Leave early
- Sensory management – earplugs, music, lavender scent, stress ball, etc.

Schedule 'free' days

- Even if you feel OK, insist on having 'free' days

MOST PEOPLE WITH ASD HAVE GOOD INTENTIONS AND JUST WANT "TO LIKE AND BE LIKED!"

JUST REMEMBER EVERYONE IS DIFFERENT...

...BUT THERE'S NO REASON YOU CAN'T MEET HALFWAY. IT JUST TAKES SOME EFFORT AND UNDERST-ANDING ON BOTH PARTS

NT/ASD

NT/NT

ASD/ASD

Many thanks for reading

Other books in The Visual Guides series at the time of writing:

The Visual Guide to Asperger's Syndrome: Meltdowns and Shutdowns

The Visual Guide to Asperger's Syndrome in 5-8 Year Olds

The Visual Guide to Asperger's Syndrome in 8-11 Year Olds

The Visual Guide to Asperger's Syndrome in 13-16 Year Olds

The Visual Guide to Asperger's Syndrome for the Neurotypical Partner

The Visual Guide to Asperger's Syndrome and Anxiety

New titles are continually being produced so keep an eye out!